WELLSPRING

21 Devotions for Your Creative Journey

Kathy Bruins & Victoria Chapin

THE WELL

PUBLISHERS

Publisher: The Well Publishers
              info@thewellpublishers.com

Editing/Editor: Kathy Bruins

Cover Design: Victoria Chapin

Table of Contents

Introduction

This devotional was born in quiet moments.

Not from a planning session or a publishing goal, but from time intentionally set aside with the Lord. In the stillness of personal devotion, a gentle awareness kept surfacing—creatives need space. Not space to perform or produce, but space to listen. Space to slow down. Space to meet with God without expectation or pressure.

As creatives, we often live in motion. We create, serve, encourage, and give of ourselves in countless ways. And while creativity is a gift from God, it can also become something we carry heavily if we are not regularly returning to Him for renewal. During these quiet moments, a desire formed to create something that would invite creatives back into intentional time with the Lord— something that would guide them into Scripture, prayer, and reflection without rushing the process.

The idea was simple: a devotional that encourages creatives to pause each day, open their Bibles, and spend unhurried time with Father, Son, and Holy Spirit. A devotional that leaves room to reflect honestly, to write prayers, to ask questions, and to listen for God's voice. One that honors the creative process by allowing space rather than filling every moment with words.

When this idea was first spoken aloud, it was shared during a phone conversation. As the vision was described, something unexpected happened. On the other end of the line, Kathy shared that she had been sensing the same prompting from the Holy Spirit. There had been no prior discussion, no coordination, and no shared planning—only confirmation that God was leading both of us toward the same invitation.

That moment became a turning point.

This devotional came to life as a shared act of obedience, shaped by prayer, Scripture, and lived experience. Together, we recognized that many creatives wrestle with similar themes—seasons of waiting, questions of calling, the need for healing, the challenge of obedience, and the desire for meaningful community. This book was written to meet creatives in those places.

Each devotion in this book follows the same rhythm, and that rhythm is intentional. We encourage you to engage with this devotional slowly. Find a quiet place where you can be fully present. Open your Bible and read the Scripture passages carefully. Take time to read before and after the verses provided so you can understand the broader context of God's Word. Scripture is not meant to be skimmed; it is meant to be entered.

Throughout these pages, you will find space to write. Use it freely. Write out your reflections, your questions, and your prayers. If a prayer offered in the devotion resonates with you, allow it to become your own—expand it, rewrite it, or continue the conversation with God in your own words. This space is yours.

This is not a devotional that you need to do daily. You do it as you have some time to relax and reflect on the goodness of God.

This devotional is written by two voices, but it ultimately points toward One. Our hope is that as you spend time in these pages, your relationship with God will deepen and your creative life will be gently shaped by time spent in His presence. May you find encouragement, clarity, and renewal as you return again and again to the place where creativity and faith are nurtured together.

You are invited to slow down here, listen, and allow God to meet you in the midst of your creative journey.

Welcome to *WellSpring*.

Victoria

1

Made in His Image

So God created human beings in his own image. In the image of God he created them; male and female he created them. — Genesis 1:27

Have you ever heard someone say, "I'm not that creative"? Or have you, yourself, made that claim?

If so, I'm right there with you. I've learned that sometimes people disqualify themselves from creativity because they don't think they're good at art, music, acting, etc. But creativity did not begin with talent. It began with God.

Before our Creator spoke light into darkness, He must have imagined it. Before stars were named and oceans were formed, He had a design. God's Word opens with creation, followed by this powerful truth: You were made in His image. That means creativity is not something reserved for a few. It is woven into every human being, including YOU!

Creativity shows up in more ways than we think. It's how we solve problems and communicate, how we express love to God and others, and how we dream about what could be.

You don't have to *feel* creative to *be* creative. You already are, because if you know Jesus, the Creator lives in you through the Holy Spirit.

Throughout Scripture, God used ordinary people in unexpected ways. Moses didn't think he could speak. David was just a shepherd, but he played the harp beautifully. God delights in awakening creativity in people who never thought it belonged to them or would be used to share His message.

You may be unsure of your gifts or too wounded to recognize them, but that doesn't mean they aren't there just waiting to burst through. The same God who formed the universe intentionally formed you— with gifts and purpose. When you express your creativity, you express your inheritance.

For we are God's masterpiece. He has created us anew in Christ Jesus, so we can do the good things he planned for us long ago. — Ephesians 2:10

Victoria

When have I believed the lie that I'm not creative?

_____

_____

_____

_____

_____

_____

_____

_____

_____

The same God who formed the universe intentionally formed you—with gifts and purpose.

What truth from God's Word speaks against that lie?

_____

_____

_____

_____

_____

_____

_____

_____

_____

_____

Prayer

Creator God, help me see myself the way You see me. Heal the places where fear, comparison, or past wounds have silenced my creativity. Awaken what You placed inside me long ago. I offer You my creativity, whatever form it takes, as worship. Use it for Your glory and to draw others to You. Amen.

2

God Makes Our Life with Purpose

For God's gifts and his call can never be withdrawn.

— Romans 11:29

How did this happen? One moment in life when I truly felt untalented: I was working in safe administrative jobs at banks and organizations, and the next thing I knew, I was speaking in front of people. Totally uncomfortable to me. But God. I began a drama team at our church that traveled to other churches. I became the prayer leader at my church, later serving as the denominational prayer leader, where I again led large groups in prayer. Then I took my writing seriously and decided to go professional. My first professional job was at a publisher of church curriculum, where I created content for elementary-age students. This project lasted three years. During that time, I was hired as a ghostwriter for a celebrity, working on multiple projects over many years. I became the president of a writing critique group in Michigan, and I was asked to write stories for a newspaper on human trafficking, which I knew little about but learned a lot about, and I became part of a team to fight it.

The story goes on and on. This devo is not about me. It's about what God does when He gifts His followers with talents, and they are obedient to go forward with those talents to give Him glory in kingdom work.

Life is exciting with God. Don't miss out on what He has for you to do for Him by using the gifts He has given you. You can't give them back ... they're yours.

God also testified to it by signs, wonders and various miracles, and by gifts of the Holy Spirit distributed according to his will.

— Hebrews 2:4

Kathy

How do I envision my life if I let God take full control? What fears do I face in surrendering everything to Him?

_____

_____

_____

_____

_____

_____

_____

_____

_____

It's about what God does when He gifts His followers with talents, and they are obedient to go forward with those talents to give Him glory in kingdom work.

Am I willing to try to give God control so I can taste and see that God is good? (Psalm 34:8)

_____

_____

_____

_____

_____

_____

_____

_____

_____

_____

Prayer

Lord, thank you for the gifts you have given me to live the purposeful life you have set before me. There is no age limit on your gifts. My life is so much more than I ever expected because of You. May I forever be guided by Your Holy Spirit in serving You. Amen.

3

When Creativity Becomes Holy Ground

Look, I have specifically chosen Bezalel, son of Uri, grandson of Hur, of the tribe of Judah. I have filled him with the Spirit of God, giving him great wisdom, ability, and expertise in all kinds of crafts.

— Exodus 31:2–3

Have you ever wondered how God will use your creativity to share the gospel … especially when your craft doesn't consist of words? Some messages are painted, illustrated, composed, or even built. No matter the medium, they are fashioned for a purpose long before they're understood.

Today, I reflected on Bezalel from the tribe of Judah and how he was chosen by God —not to preach or teach, but to create. Scripture tells us that God specifically filled him with the Spirit, giving him divine wisdom and exceptional skills to construct the tabernacle. Bezalel helped create a sacred space where God would dwell among His people.

Those who entered that space may not have known why certain designs—colors, textures, and fabrics—stirred their hearts, but God knew what would give them joy and cause them to fall on their faces in praise. He used Bezalel's Spirit-prompted creativity to bring the Israelites into awe of His glorious presence.

When the Holy Spirit leads creativity, it becomes more than art. It becomes holy ground. That is often how God works through creatives, making places for His people to encounter Him still today.

If you sense the Holy Spirit prompting you to create something without fully knowing why, perhaps it's an invitation to trust, lean in, and carry it through. Our creator sees the full picture, including those who will encounter His presence through your offering of obedience.

It is the one and only Spirit who distributes all these gifts. He alone decides which gift each person should have. — 1 Corinthians 12:11

Victoria

When have I felt prompted to create without fully knowing why?

_____

_____

_____

_____

_____

_____

_____

_____

_____

_____

**When the Holy Spirit leads
creativity, it becomes more
than art. It becomes
holy ground.**

How might God use that work to bring another closer to Him?

_____

_____

_____

_____

_____

_____

_____

_____

_____

_____

Prayer

Holy Spirit, teach me to listen and respond when You prompt me to create. Help me trust You even when I don't understand the purpose. Use my creativity to prepare holy ground where others can encounter You. May my work be led by You and offered back for kingdom purpose. Amen.

4

Perfecting Your Plan through God's Steps

We can make our plans, but the Lord determines our steps. — Proverbs 16:9

How did you plan your life? Was it the influence of parents or friends that determined your steps? Perhaps you've been following someone on social media who has done well with their life's work, and it's similar to what you think you would like to do. You focus on what they do and may find yourself imitating it. Is that what God wants for you?

The world offers so much to individuals, some good and some not great. You want to make sure that the time, money, and energy you invest in developing who you want to be and what you want to do are trustworthy. To put a plan in place for your life without the Lord's guidance is like hiking without a compass … it's easy to get lost.

Scams are run on your desires. I was the victim of a scam while looking for a writing job online. It sounded so perfect for me. Then some things they said didn't seem right. I said I didn't agree. They said, "What do you mean?" I said, "This sounds like a scam." They hung up. Scammers pull you in with what you want to hear and rob you of money, time, identification, or more.

If a person takes the wrong path that leads them to what seems like the perfect direction, they may find nothing of value when they arrive. It's really sad when someone near the end of their life realizes they missed out on what they really should have been doing.

The Lord will give you chance after chance to pick up on His message of what you are to do, but if you're not in tune with God, you will most likely miss it. It takes deliberate, intentional steps to hear the voice of the Lord in your life. You need to talk to God about everything; that's what friends do. They build on their relationship. God does know all about you, and He invites you to learn more about Him every day.

Create a space where you and Jesus can meet daily. He is faithful to join you there every day because He loves you and wants to spend time with you.

For I know the plans I have for you," declares the Lord, "plans to prosper you and not to harm you, plans to give you hope and a future.

—Jeremiah 29:11

Kathy

20

What is one thing I would like to change in my life, and why?

_____

_____

_____

_____

_____

_____

_____

_____

_____

_____

To put a plan in place for your life without the Lord's guidance is like hiking without a compass … it's easy to get lost.

What changes would be beneficial for me? What do I feel God is telling me?

_____

_____

_____

_____

_____

_____

_____

_____

_____

_____

Prayer

Jesus, take my hand and lead me to what You want me to do. Enlighten me with Your Word. Correct me when I take a wrong turn and put me back on the path meant for me. Amen.

5

Audience of One

Work willingly at whatever you do, as though you were working for the Lord rather than for people.

— Colossians 3:23

Today, as I was writing, some questions came to mind. *What if this were only for God? What if no one else ever saw it, applauded it, or even understood it? Would it still be worth doing?*

Scripture reminds us that whatever we do, we are to do it as unto the Lord. Creativity is no exception. When we create for Him first, our work becomes more than expression or skill. It becomes an offering, a giving back of what He has already given to us.

David understood this kind of devotion. Long before he stepped into the role of a king or a psalmist, he was a shepherd worshiping God in the fields. His songs were born from love, not recognition. He created because he adored God, and was a man after God's own heart.

Our creativity can reflect that same posture. When we offer our gifts to God first, our relationship with

Him becomes more intimate. We draw closer. We listen more carefully. We create not to impress, but to pour out love and devotion to our Heavenly Father.

God, in His faithfulness, then opens doors of opportunity for our creative works to bless others. But even if it were only for Him, it would be enough. He is the most worthy audience.

May we be men and women after God's heart, offering our creativity back to Him in love.

Take delight in the Lord, and he will give you your heart's desires. — Psalm 37:4

Victoria

What would change if I created with God as my first and only audience?

_____

_____

_____

_____

_____

_____

_____

_____

_____

_____

We create not to impress, but to pour out love and devotion to our Heavenly Father.

How might my creativity deepen my relationship with Him?

_____

_____

_____

_____

_____

_____

_____

_____

_____

Prayer

Heavenly Father, help me remember that You are my first audience. Holy Spirit, teach me to have a heart that creates as an offering of Christ's love, not for my own recognition or approval. To You be all the glory. May my creativity draw me closer to You and reflect a heart devoted to You above all else. Amen.

6

It's All God's:
The Beginning of The Well

Now all glory to God, who is able, through his mighty power at work within us, to accomplish infinitely more than we might ask or think. Glory to him in the church and in Christ Jesus through all generations forever and ever! Amen.

— Ephesians 3:20-21

I love doing ministry because that's when I truly see and feel God at work. I am addicted to that feeling, and it is so good. I never tire of it.

When we started meeting as a leadership team for The Well, I knew the call was huge, yet I also knew that God made the call, and nothing is impossible… He can do anything. I admit that at times I was nervous about getting a venue, speakers, faculty, and what felt like a million other details together. The team and I always prayed, thanking God for the vision and asking for help, knowing He would provide—and He did in miraculous ways.

I remember the first emails and phone calls I made to get keynotes and faculty. I believed they would never want to be a part of this unknown venture with a relatively unknown leader. This is what I call faulty thinking, which may have come from old files in my mind from childhood or from the evil one. I just knew it wasn't from God.

Imagine my delight when a venue emerged, keynotes and faculty said yes, and the leadership team grew to include important parts of the puzzle. It was more than I imagined. God went before me, preparing hearts and minds for what I was proposing. It wasn't the money we would pay people; starting out, we had very little. It was the call of God that made the difference among all these individuals. The Well was established because it's God's ministry, and I'm so thankful that I was called to be a part of it.

There are different kinds of service, but the same Lord. There are different kinds of working, but in all of them and in everyone it is the same God at work. Now to each one the manifestation of the Spirit is given for the common good. – 1 Corinthians 12:5-7

Where have I seen God at work through my gifts or at The Well (if attended)?

_____

_____

_____

_____

_____

_____

_____

_____

_____

_____

It was the call of God that made the difference among all these individuals.

What has that taught me about myself in a relationship with God?

_____

_____

_____

_____

_____

_____

_____

_____

_____

_____

Prayer

God, I cannot thank you enough for The Well. Your fingerprints are all over it. You have blessed so many creatives with Your presence in their lives, and You met us all at The Well. Amen.

7

Created for Community

Two people are better off than one, for they can help each other succeed. — Ecclesiastes 4:9

The creative journey can sometimes feel lonely, especially when it seems like your calling doesn't fit neatly into a familiar box. You may wonder if anyone truly understands the weight you carry or the vision God placed in your heart.

Even when surrounded by people, it's possible to feel isolated and unsure of where you belong. But God's Word teaches us that we were never meant to walk alone. He designed us for relationships—with Jesus first and then with one another.

In 2018, I was one of the very first attendees at The Well Conference for creatives. I was finally ready to take the next step in writing a book about my daughter, Sydney, who died in 2008. A slew of butterflies filled my stomach. I was both excited and nervous since I didn't know what to expect.

Who knew when I walked through those doors, a whole new world would open up for me? Although I was overwhelmed, I felt seen and understood. I rubbed shoulders with my newfound people and learned so much. Lasting friendships were formed, and The Well became my community. Now I lead that ministry and conference. God knew exactly what I needed.

Not only do we need safe spaces where gifts are nurtured, but also where faith is strengthened as iron sharpens iron. We grow when we are heard and encouraged. Sometimes God uses others to remind us of truth when we're too tired to speak it ourselves.

Jesus surrounded Himself with others as He walked out His ministry. Community was His Father's divine plan. Now we are called to be co-laborers with Christ in spreading God's mission. We are to be agents of reconciliation, collaborating to bring the world back to Him through our gifts.

If you've been trying to carry your calling on your own, here is your invitation to lean in and find the strength and refreshment found in shared purpose. Together, let's embrace the blessings of people who walk with us, pray with us, and celebrate with us in the essential, beautiful gift of community.

So encourage each other and build each other up, just as you are already doing.

— 1 Thessalonians 5:11

When have I felt isolated in my creative journey?

_____

_____

_____

_____

_____

_____

_____

_____

_____

_____

**We are to be agents of reconciliation,
collaborating to bring the world back
to Him through our gifts.**

Who might God be inviting me to walk alongside in this season?

_____

_____

_____

_____

_____

_____

_____

_____

_____

_____

Prayer

Heavenly Father, thank You for creating me for relationship and community. If I've been walking alone out of fear, pride, or weariness, help me open my heart to the people You've placed around me. Show me where You are inviting me to connect, grow, and be encouraged as I fulfill Your assignments for my life. In Jesus' name, Amen.

8

Watching Over
Your Possessions

Now, a person who is put in charge as a manager must be faithful. — 1 Corinthians 4:2

Stewardship means to manage or look after (another's property). What does this mean to creatives? Think about your talents, possessions, health, family, etc., that are a part of your life. Where did all these come from? You may think that you worked on your talent to make it good, made money to buy possessions, exercise every day to be healthy, and so on. All of these are good things to do, but ultimately, they came from God. Psalm 24:1 says, "The earth is the Lord's, and everything in it."

God's gifts have purpose. First Peter 4:10 states, "Each of you should use whatever gift you have received to serve others, as faithful stewards of God's grace in its various forms." You are a blessing to others by using your gifts to help, encourage, direct, teach, and serve in other ways. Mainly, you bless God by giving Him the glory of your gift. Remember to manage and take care of the gifts God gives you. He is trusting you as a faithful servant. Don't bury your talents but multiply them by the power of the Holy Spirit.

How could your talents multiply? Could you use it to bless someone in need? That is a blessing to others as well who witness your gift.

How can you protect your character in the use of your gift? What safeguards could you put in place to use your gift in a trustworthy manner? Satan wants you to fail and show the world how God's people can't be trusted. Don't fall for his tricks. Hold tight to Jesus, and He will bring you to safety in all you do.

Each of you should use whatever gift you have received to serve others, as faithful stewards of God's grace in its various forms. — 1 Peter 4:10

Which talent that I have do I like best? Why is that?

_____

_____

_____

_____

_____

_____

_____

_____

_____

_____

_____

Satan wants you to fail and show the world how God's people can't be trusted.

How can I multiply it to bless many?

_____

_____

_____

_____

_____

_____

_____

_____

_____

Prayer

God, I am amazed at how much you have blessed me. I pray that these blessings will be put to good use in fulfilling Your purpose for me. May I not take them for granted but uphold them for all to see what You can do. Let me be Your hands, feet, mouth, and more for Your glory. Amen.

9

Your Story is Ministry

And they have defeated him by the blood of the Lamb and by their testimony. — Revelation 12:11a

Have you ever wondered if your story really matters? Maybe you've thought, *Who would want to hear this, anyway?* Or, *I don't have it all figured out yet.* Perhaps you've assumed your story isn't dramatic enough, polished enough, or complete enough to be useful to God.

But Scripture tells us that testimony carries power. Not because our stories are perfect, but because they point to a faithful God at work in our lives.

God has always used ordinary people and personal stories to share His truth. The Samaritan woman didn't have a theological degree or a cleaned-up past. She simply told others what Jesus had done for her, and many in her town came to believe.

Your story doesn't need to be figured out to impact the world. In fact, the Lord often uses what we share in the process to bring hope to someone else who's stuck. The very places you've wrestled, waited, or healed may become the places where others recognize God's grace.

As creatives, we often share our lived experiences through art, words, music, and film. When offered to God, these expressions become ministry. They open hearts, create connection, and welcome others to encounter Jesus.

You don't have to share everything, and you don't have to share all at once. As the Holy Spirit leads, your obedience to tell your story, in whatever form it takes, becomes a powerful witness.

God will guide those who hear it. Your role is simply to offer it. Your story matters because all the days of your life were written before any of them took shape. And the Divine Author will use it in ways you may never fully see.

You saw me before I was born. Every day of my life was recorded in your book. Every moment was laid out before a single day had passed.

— Psalm 139:16.

Victoria

What part of my story might God be inviting me to share in this season?

_____

_____

_____

_____

_____

_____

_____

_____

_____

_____

Your story matters because all the days of your life were written before any of them took shape.

How could my creativity help tell that story in a way that points others to Him?

_____

_____

_____

_____

_____

_____

_____

_____

_____

_____

Prayer

Father God, thank You for authoring my life story. Help me trust You with it, even the hard and unfinished parts. Give me discernment to know when and how to share and courage to be obedient when You prompt me. Use my story to point others to You and bring hope where it's needed most. Amen.

10

Fearless Speaking of Truth

This is my command—be strong and courageous! Do not be afraid or discouraged. For the Lord your God is with you wherever you go. — Joshua 1:9

Speaking in front of people can be difficult, especially when the subject is tricky. If you've been in those shoes, you know what I am talking about. There are fears, real or not, you need to work through. What if I don't say the right words? People may get mad at the topic. Some words push buttons, and people react. God has an answer for all these fears that you may experience.

I experienced that while leading a large retreat. In my talk, I knew God wanted me to talk about my anxiety disorder. I didn't want to. The day of the talk, God and I wrestled until 4:00 a.m. Guess who won? Yes, I chose obedience. When I started talking about my anxiety disorder, one woman ran from the room, a few minutes later, another lady left, and one other woman was crying at her table. The pastor told me later that these ladies were all dealing with the same issues I shared. God knew what He was doing.

Fearlessness comes from God. You know what God has called you to speak on, and you accepted the call. God made your mouth (Exodus 4:11) and will give you the words to say. The Lord will not leave you hanging. His Spirit will rise up in you and take over the talk. Of course, preparation to speak is necessary, but the Spirit goes beyond what you plan and practice. It truly is a powerful moment that you will not want to miss.

Why must you do this? Because God said so? It's more than that. It's because the Lord has given you a divine purpose in your life. Part of that purpose is to speak truth at all times, not just when you're up on the stage. There are people who are literally dying to hear those words of truth. God's Word saves.

Will you trust God with the words you will say and rely on Him to give you the courage you need? Pray for the wisdom, strength, and joy of serving the Lord in this way. Let your faith shine brightly for all to see.

Be strong and courageous. Do not be afraid or terrified because of them, for the Lord your God goes with you; he will never leave you nor forsake you. — Deuteronomy 31:6

44

What do I love about speaking?

_____

_____

_____

_____

_____

_____

_____

_____

_____

_____

**There are people who are literally
dying to hear those words of truth.**

What is my favorite type of speaking? How do I see You use it?

_____

_____

_____

_____

_____

_____

_____

_____

_____

Prayer

Most Holy God, thank you for the opportunity to speak truth to others, knowing Your words will draw them closer to You. I pray that the words I speak will give freedom and life to many. May Your courage and love reign in me as I perform this task. Lord, I ask you to empower my speaking. You can do great things. I am Your servant. Amen.

11

Comparison Dries the Well

There are different kinds of spiritual gifts, but the same Spirit is the source of them all

— 1 Corinthians 12:4

Oh Lord, I don't like this feeling, I thought, as a fellow creative was celebrating her success. "I should be happy for her," I whispered.

Ever happen to you? I'm not proud to write this, but I'm thankful for the Holy Spirit's conviction that led me to Jesus' teachings on humility. Praise the Lord that I no longer carry that angst.

Comparison has a way of creeping in. Instead of developing the gifts the Lord instilled in us, we sometimes measure ourselves against others. If we let it, coveting interrupts our creative flow and leaves our well dry.

Scripture reminds us that comparison pulls our focus away from serving others and places it on performance and approval. God doesn't expect us to create like everyone else. He wants us to be faithful with what He's entrusted us.

Throughout His Word, He used people whose purpose and calling varied. One of David's ministries was music, while Paul communicated through letters. Peter preached boldly to crowds. Each carried the message of the Gospel in a way that fit them, their circumstances, and those they'd encounter to share it with.

Your story and style matter. Your ministry is uniquely yours. The more you embrace your purpose and calling, the more you will find the peace of Christ. Your heart will be filled with joy for others, and celebration will abound. Creativity is more likely to come, and your well will be filled to overflowing.

And let the peace that comes from Christ rule in your hearts. For as members of one body, you are called to live in peace. And always be thankful.

— Colossians 3:15

Victoria

Where has comparison influenced how I view my creativity?

_____

_____

_____

_____

_____

_____

_____

_____

_____

_____

The more you embrace your purpose and calling, the more you will find the peace of Christ.

What can I do to celebrate another creative today?

_____

_____

_____

_____

_____

_____

_____

_____

_____

Prayer

Father God, forgive me for the times I've allowed comparison to slow the creativity You've placed within me. Help me keep my eyes on You, my Source. Teach me to create from obedience to serve, not from insecurity and the need for approval. Restore my confidence in the call You've given me, so I can celebrate what You're doing in me and, most importantly, in others. In Jesus' name, Amen.

12

Patience Helps in Most Cases

But those who trust in the Lord will find new strength. They will soar high on wings like eagles. They will run and not grow weary. They will walk and not faint. — Isaiah 40:31

Have you ever moved ahead in a situation the way you wanted it to be when someone didn't respond to your question right away? How did that go? I have done that, and it usually ends in disaster. People think that I am trying to control the situation. They believe that I have no consideration for their thoughts or feelings. It's just not good. I slap my forehead and wonder why I didn't wait for the person to answer. I know it's hard to wait, but we can get further ahead if we do. If we move forward without the answer needed, we are running ahead of the Lord. He knows all about it and is working on it. We must trust Him to do what is needed for us to move forward in His power.

What are some ways we can be patient? We can work on something else to get our minds off it. You could make a list of the pros and cons, or other possible solutions, that we will have ready when the person responds. We could be creative and make something just for ourselves that reminds us to be patient. Perhaps dig into the Scriptures about patience and list them.

What happens when we wait on the Lord? He works through us, giving new strength, and we will not tire. We will be refreshed and ready to take on the task completing it. If we don't wait, we are moving blindly through the task to what we think it should be. When we wait on circumstances, the Lord is at work. He is always working and doesn't give up.

For it is God who is working in you, enabling you both to desire and to work out His good purpose.
— Philippians 2:13

Kathy

What can I do when I am not patient?

_____

_____

_____

_____

_____

_____

_____

_____

_____

_____

What happens when we wait on the Lord? He works through us, giving new strength, and we will not tire.

Search a website like Bible Gateway for the words patience/patient. What does God say we should do?

_____

_____

_____

_____

_____

_____

_____

_____

_____

_____

Prayer

Lord, thank you for always working on my behalf. I can trust you to do what is needed and give me the direction I need to go. Help me to wait, I pray. Amen.

13

God Tends to the Wounded Places

He heals the brokenhearted and bandages their wounds. — Psalm 147:3

Creativity, like grief, is not linear. It presents differently, depending on the person and the circumstances. Sometimes the wounds inspire us; at other times, they stop us in our tracks. It's unpredictable.

When my daughter met Jesus face-to-face just before her 15th birthday, I knew immediately that I would still write the book we planned to write together. While I was moved to do so, sitting down to work on it has brought hours and hours of tears.

Loss, trauma, and disappointment are painful to approach and can interrupt our creative flow in ways we find hard to control. Creating can stir memories we'd rather avoid, and procrastination can feel safer than expression.

God sees these tender places. His Word tells us that He is a healer of broken hearts. He does not rush us through our grief nor ask us to pretend it doesn't exist. Instead, He meets us where we are, and the Holy Spirit gently helps us process in ways we might not have words for yet.

If your creativity feels fragile, it may be the Lord welcoming you into a season of restoration. This isn't a setback. It's our Savior's care for you. He knows that His gifts flow best from a heart that feels safe, tended, and loved.

Healing doesn't happen all at once. Sometimes it comes slowly, layer by layer. You don't need to push through pain. Surrender it and give yourself permission to lament.

Nothing entrusted to Him is ever lost. Our Father in heaven is faithful to restore what has been wounded. Healing will come, and as it does, creativity will follow in beautiful ways that line up with your destiny.

The Lord is close to the brokenhearted; he rescues those whose spirits are crushed. — Psalm 34:18

Victoria

Has pain or loss affected my creativity? If so, in what way?

_____

_____

_____

_____

_____

_____

_____

_____

_____

_____

If your creativity feels fragile, it may be the Lord welcoming you into a season of restoration.

What would it look like to invite God into my healing process today?

_____

_____

_____

_____

_____

_____

_____

_____

_____

_____

Prayer

Father God, You see the places in my heart that have been hurt or broken. I invite You into those places today. Heal any pain that has interrupted my creativity, and restore what feels fragile. Help me trust You with my work as You tend to my heart. I receive Your care and Your timing. In Jesus' name, Amen.

14

Raise Your Hands to the Lord

May the kindness of the Lord our God be upon us; and confirm for us the work of our hands: Yes, confirm the work of our hands.

— Psalm 90:17 (NASB)

Can you imagine how difficult, not impossible, life would be without hands? There are many in the world without hands who live normal lives, accomplishing incredible feats by finding other ways to do what hands do. I admire their creativity and their steadfastness in getting things done. In fact, it should inspire us to use our hands more in daily life. Things that we take for granted in having hands, we never give a thought to doing.

What would you do with your hands that would be out of the ordinary in your normal routine? You are creative, so you can come up with many new ways to use your hands. Perhaps pray about it first and see what the Lord lays on your heart.

The gift of hands makes life easier for most to do what God has put on their hearts. Whether it is writing, acting, painting, or more, it is what makes the task come to be. Our hands and feet are what Jesus uses to accomplish many things for Him. Jesus isn't here in the physical to hug a person, but we can hug them for Jesus. When we write a story, we use a pen and paper, or we hit many keys on a laptop. What's written has a purpose for many or maybe a few. The plans for all we do and create are God's. We are to be obedient to them. There are infinite possibilities.

We want to serve Jesus with our gifts. The confirmation of doing that comes from the blessing for the person(s) being served, along with our own blessing in knowing God appoints us for such a time. You feel God's approval in your heart, and it feels so good.

Whatever your hand finds to do, do it with all your might. — Ecclesiastes 9:10

What could I do with my hands that I haven't done before?

_____

_____

_____

_____

_____

_____

_____

_____

_____

_____

Jesus isn't here in the physical to hug a person, but we can hug them for Jesus.

How can I worship God with my hands?

_____

_____

_____

_____

_____

_____

_____

_____

_____

_____

_____

Prayer

Lord, we thank you for hands. Many of our gifts need them to produce what You have set our hearts and minds to do. Help us to see how we can reach people for You in using our hands … and our feet … and our voices. Amen.

15

The Sacred Pause

Be still and know that I am God. — Psalm 46:10

Have you ever sat with your creativity and felt ... nothing? I have. No inspiration. No clear direction. Just empty and discouraged, wondering why the well has run dry.

The answers don't come when I want them to, although I continue to pray. I wait, but nothing appears to be moving, and God seems like He's way off in the distance. You too?

I've learned there are seasons when creativity doesn't rush forward and overflow. Instead, it slows ... pauses. The ideas seem out of reach, and the joy in creating is lost. It can leave us questioning whether we've missed something or somehow lost what God once gave us.

What if that stillness and waiting are not signs of absence, but invitations instead? Even though we can't sense Him at times, God is always present. Perhaps silence is His way of drawing us closer, inviting us to listen more deeply and trust more fully.

In 1 Kings 19:11-19, I'm reminded that Elijah didn't hear God in the wind, the earthquake, or fire, but in a gentle whisper. He went through those loud, obvious happenings, yet leaned in to hear God in the quiet. Pressing in seasons are not empty seasons. Perhaps they are forming seasons.

When creativity feels stalled, it doesn't mean your gift has disappeared. It may mean God is tending the well beneath the surface. Roots are growing. Faith is being strengthened. Dependence on Him is deepening. Sometimes, the work God is doing in us is more important than the work He is doing through us.

The flow will return, because God is faithful. Until then, rest in the truth that He is still at work, even when you cannot see it.

The Lord is good to those who depend on him, to those who search for him. So it is good to wait quietly for salvation from the Lord.

— Lamentations 3: 25-26

Where do I feel discouraged or stuck right now?

_____

_____

_____

_____

_____

_____

_____

_____

_____

**Sometimes, the work God is doing
in us is more important than the
work He is doing through us.**

What might God be forming in me during this quiet season?

_____

_____

_____

_____

_____

_____

_____

_____

_____

_____

Prayer

Father God, when my creativity feels quiet and my heart feels discouraged, help me trust You in the stillness. Teach me to wait patiently and listen closely. Restore what feels dry, and strengthen me in this season of listening for You. I place my hope in You, my never-ending Source. Amen.

16

Get Enthused

So whether you eat or drink, or whatever you do, do it all for the glory of God. — 1 Corinthians 10:31

Have you ever gotten a job or a volunteer position that uses your creative gifts that you were genuinely excited about? You can't wait to get started, and you dream about all that may happen. You start and it is a wonderful experience. Then the honeymoon is over, and you find that not all things about the position are great anymore. In fact, parts of it may be difficult or downright boring. However, you must do these items to be successful at your job. You can't ignore them because somewhere down the road, it will be noticed that it wasn't done, and you will be called to account for it. That usually isn't a pleasant time. That happens to most of us who start a new job. But how can we move through it?

We need to backtrack and remember why we were so excited at the beginning. We are using our gifts for the Lord. All the work we do ultimately is for the Lord. Would we look at the task with the same eyes knowing that Christ is counting on us to do a good job? The words we write and speak, will they still come from our heart of creative passion? You are serving the Lord in all you do. Make it the best you have to offer, for this will glorify God. Your job will have more meaning for you, too.

Do your best to present yourself to God as one approved, a worker who does not need to be ashamed and who correctly handles the word of truth. —2 Timothy 2:15

Kathy

What are some things that excite me about my work?

_____

_____

_____

_____

_____

_____

_____

_____

_____

_____

Would we look at the task with the same eyes knowing that Christ is counting on us to do a good job?

When my day gets challenging, what can I do to feel uplifted again?

_____

_____

_____

_____

_____

_____

_____

_____

_____

_____

Prayer

Gracious God who knows what our innermost desires are, You give great gifts to Your children. The jobs and positions we have are important to You and need to be vital to us. I pray we can give our full passion and energy to the tasks given to us. We love to serve You. We want to honor You. Amen.

17

When Faithfulness Feels Risky

And this same God who takes care of me will supply all your needs from his glorious riches, which have been given to us in Christ Jesus.

— Philippians 4:19

Has your creative journey, like mine, come to a point where the questions become very practical? Can I afford to keep going? Is this ministry work sustainable?

Many creatives long to serve God fully with their gifts, yet feel the tension of real-life responsibilities. Bills still need to be paid, and families provided for. Dreams don't always come with clear provision. Faithfulness to the call can begin to feel risky.

I took the leap of faith to volunteer full-time with The Well Ministry after my layoff from the corporate world in June of 2020. It hasn't been easy financially, but God's provision has arrived in ways I didn't expect. It was the waiting and putting my hand to the plow that led to unexpected connections with paid work outside of my volunteer role. God is so good!

As I've continued to fast and pray over this, I've been reminded that God is aware of my needs. Not only is He the Giver of my gifts, but the Provider who sustains me. I will keep trusting Him one step at a time as I've learned from some of the best.

In Genesis and Hebrews, you'll find that Abraham left what was familiar. Moses stepped into leadership with uncertainty in the book of Exodus. And in multiple places in Acts, we see that Paul continued in obedience even when the provision looked slim in the natural. None of them had the full picture, but they trusted the One who did.

If you're in a tug of war between your creative calling and practical needs, know that faith grows in this tension. Place what God has entrusted you with back into His hands. He honors faithfulness, even when it feels costly.

Commit your actions to the Lord, and your plans will succeed. — Proverbs 16:3

Victoria

When does being a good steward of God's gifts feel risky for me?

_____

_____

_____

_____

_____

_____

_____

_____

_____

If you're in a tug of war between your creative calling and practical needs, know that faith grows in this tension.

What would it look like to trust God with both my calling and my provision?

_____

_____

_____

_____

_____

_____

_____

_____

_____

_____

Prayer

Father God, You know the responsibilities I carry and the desires You've placed in my heart. Help me trust You with both. Teach me to walk in obedience without fear, believing that You will provide what I need in supernatural ways and in Your perfect timing. I place my calling and finances into Your hands. In the mighty name of Jesus, Amen.

18

Faith that is Confident

Faith shows the reality of what we hope for; it is the evidence of things we cannot see. — Hebrews 11:1

When I was a child, I remember my family receiving a Christmas catalog from a store with lots of toys. I would study, list, and turn the corners on pages to everything I hoped for … and it was a lot. The catalog looked well-used by the time Christmas was done. I was always thrilled with whatever I received, and it was nowhere near all that I chose in the catalog. I knew that I wouldn't get everything, and that was okay.

As an adult who is creative, I still have lists of things I hope for. My prayer list holds many items on my heart, but it's different than my Christmas list because I know Whom I am asking. I know that He is the Creator of all things and holds all things in His hands. There is confidence in this.

I am confident that God hears my prayers and that He will answer them. I know that His way is best. He creates more than I can imagine in my prayers and answers them many times in surprising ways.

This is because He sees the big picture while I only see what's around me. There is so much in this world that I cannot see, but when answers come from my prayers, it is proof that God is taking action, and my faith grows in response. Even if it's not what I thought the answer should be, I have confidence that it is real and the best.

The prayer of a righteous person is powerful and effective. — James 5:16

What are some prayers that I have been praying for a long time?

_____

_____

_____

_____

_____

_____

_____

_____

_____

_____

He creates more than I can imagine in my prayers and answers them many times in surprising ways.

How do I feel God is answering them?

_____

_____

_____

_____

_____

_____

_____

_____

_____

Prayer

I thank You, Lord, for the many times You have acted on my prayers. Sometimes it is to change my heart, and I need to be open to that. You never let me down. Amen.

19

The Answer is, "Yes!"

It is not that we think we are qualified to do anything on our own. Our qualification comes from God.

— 2 Corinthians 3:5

Have you had times in your creative ministry when God's invitation to "do" was right in front of you, but you struggled to take the next steps? Almost immediately, questions arise. *Am I ready for this? Are you sure about this, Lord?* Obedience often asks more of us than what we're prepared to give.

I became a mom at a young age and worked part-time as a restaurant server for years. When the Lord opened a door for me to work in an office, I learned how to give an unprepared "yes." I had no formal education, so I muddled through my on-the-job training.

I didn't know then, but God was preparing me for today. Each job I've had has brought me readiness for the next, and it's carried over into my creative walk.

Looking back, I see a pattern: I said "yes" without knowing how, and the Lord opened doors for the right training, at just the right time. I've been like a swan, gliding along smoothly above water... while underneath, feet treading wildly to stay afloat!

In the Bible, God didn't wait until His people felt fully equipped before He commissioned them. The Apostle Paul articulates that Christ followers are not self-qualified for ministry. Their qualifications instead originated with the Father. When we move in obedience, divine grace is sufficient in weakness because that's where Christ's power is most effective.

If you're standing at the edge of a next step, unsure but willing, know this: Your role is obedience, and you can trust God with the outcome. When He asks, you can say, "The answer is yes, Lord. Now what is the question?"

Each time he said, "My grace is all you need. My power works best in weakness." So now I am glad to boast about my weaknesses, so that the power of Christ can work through me.

— 2 Corinthians 12:9

Victoria

How has God prepared me in the past for something He had planned for my future?

_____

_____

_____

_____

_____

_____

_____

_____

_____

When we move in obedience, divine grace is sufficient in weakness because that's where Christ's power is most effective.

Where might God be inviting me to take a step of obedience right now?

_____

_____

_____

_____

_____

_____

_____

_____

_____

_____

Prayer

Lord, when you call me forward, help me respond with trust. Give me the faith to take the next step in obedience, even when I don't feel equipped. I place the outcome in Your hands and offer You my yes. Amen.

20

Be Courageous for You are in His Grip

So do not fear, for I am with you; do not be dismayed, for I am your God. I will strengthen you and help you; I will uphold you with my righteous right hand. — Isaiah 41:10

Being courageous is hard for many, but I believe the Lord gives us opportunities to practice going forward with no fear. Standing up for what we believe in can be demonstrated through speaking, writing, art, drama, music, and more. Not everyone may agree with us. Are we okay with that, or does it scare us?

God gifts a creative for times like that. Many biblical examples, such as Moses, Esther, Joseph, and Noah, and others, who may not have been courageous at first but realized that God had control over whatever scenario was unfolding. They trusted God and became fearless. He filled them with the strength they needed to do the task.

That is true for you, too. If an opportunity arises to perform your gift in front of others, like the Celebration of the Arts at The Well, remember God called you to it and will fill you with what you need. Be brave, knowing that God is with you. He hasn't left you to fend for yourself. The gift you have will bless others and glorify God. With you telling and/or showing your talents, God's purpose is being lived out through you.

As your confidence in God grows, your gifts will grow as you release any anxiety from the past and run free with your talent to levels you've never experienced before. Stage fright will not be an issue for you, because you know you perform for One.

For God gave us a spirit not of fear but of power and love and self-control. — 2 Timothy 1:7

Kathy

What is my greatest fear in connection with my talent?

_____

_____

_____

_____

_____

_____

_____

_____

_____

_____

**Be brave, knowing that
God is with you.**

What are the Scriptures that encourage me not to be afraid?

_____

_____

_____

_____

_____

_____

_____

_____

_____

_____

_____

Prayer

Dear Lord, I pray for a heart of strength and courage to serve You as You would want me to. I pray for the Holy Spirit to quench any fear I experience and be free from it. May my heart and soul represent the Lord I trust and love. Amen.

21

Drawing from The Well

Anyone who drinks this water will soon become thirsty again. But those who drink the water I give will never be thirsty again. It becomes a fresh, bubbling spring within them, giving them eternal life.

— John 4:13–14

As creatives, we give and give. We pour out our ideas, stories, art, encouragement, and love. We show up for others even when we are tired. If we're not careful, our buckets become empty, and we realize we're trying to give from a place that's run dry.

The truth is simple, yet easy to forget. We cannot give what we do not have.

In John 4, Jesus meets a woman at a well. She knew the routine. Carry the bucket, draw the water, and return when the supply is gone. Jesus compassionately tells her that the water she's been drinking will never fully satisfy. Those who drink it will be thirsty again and again.

He offers something better. Jesus tells her that the water He gives will become a spring within her, welling up to eternal life. No more constant striving. No more dependence on an outside source that never quite satisfies. What He offers is lasting, sustaining, and alive.

We find ourselves there, don't we? We return to the "wells" of life that temporarily refresh. We rely on productivity, affirmation, or even ministry itself to fill us. But those waters alone dry up. Jesus invites us to drink deeply from His presence, to lay down our empty buckets and receive what only He can give.

Creativity was not meant to empty us. It was meant to flow through us from a life rooted in Jesus. As you answer the call to bring others to Christ through your gifts, remember this: The Well is here. Return often. Drink deeply. Be filled so you can be a joyful wellspring for the salvation of others. This is your purpose. You were created for this.

We hope to see YOU at The Well.

With joy, you will drink deeply from the fountain of salvation! — Isaiah 12:3

Victoria

When or where have I been trying to give from an empty place?

_____

_____

_____

_____

_____

_____

_____

_____

_____

_____

Creativity was not meant to empty us. It was meant to flow through us from a life rooted in Jesus.

What would it look like for me to return regularly to Jesus as my *WellSpring*?

_____

_____

_____

_____

_____

_____

_____

_____

_____

Prayer

Jesus, You see how easily I pour myself out. Forgive me for trying to give what I haven't first received from You. Draw me to You, to be filled, restored, and renewed. May my creativity flow from Your living water, becoming a wellspring of salvation to others without depleting my soul. May it bring joy to me and those You've called me to serve. In Your mighty name I pray, yes and amen.

A Closing Blessing

As you go from this place, may you go rooted in the truth that God is your Source. May you create from intimacy rather than obligation, from obedience rather than fear, and from trust rather than striving. May you remember that your gifts were given with purpose, and that the One who called you is faithful to sustain you.

May you walk forward attentive to the Holy Spirit's leading, bold in obedience, and gentle with yourself in every season. May your creativity make space for others to encounter Christ, and may you return often to be renewed by Him. You are sent, not alone, but held—commissioned to create from a life continually filled with Living Water.

In Jesus name, Amen.

Kathy Bruins

Kathy Bruins, an award-winning author, has been a professional writer since 2000. Her goal has always been to glorify God and help other writers.

Kathy was the president of the West Michigan chapter of Word Weavers Int. She founded The Well Ministry to Creatives, a 501(c)3, in 2017. In 2025, she founded The Well Publishers, an LLC ministry to help writers get published as they follow their creative journey with God.

A new talent she is growing is voice-over for audiobooks. She has her own studio in her home and enjoys creating audiobooks for clients. She is an IMDb Member.

Kathy lives in Southwest Michigan with her husband, John, and enjoys the area's seasons. Hobbies include cooking, baking, and puzzles ... she likes the hard ones.

Victoria Chapin

Victoria Chapin is an author and speaker who inspires others to find jewels in adversity and live fully in Christ. Despite the tragic loss of her daughter and enduring a rare cancer diagnosis, she is passionate about joy. Victoria embraces the truth found in John 10:10; Jesus came that we may have life in abundance.  Her writings encourage intimacy with God, equipping her readers to walk boldly in their destiny. She speaks nationally and has been featured on Christian programming and multiple podcasts.

Victoria serves as Executive Director for The Well Ministry and Conference, where she is dedicated to discipling and empowering Christian creatives. She is also a co-founder of Do Life 2 The Full Ministries, where she serves as a chaplain alongside her husband, focusing on prayer, discipleship, and community outreach. Victoria is a mom to many and Grammy to even more, who loves books and all things coffee, especially when shared with friends.

THE WELL

Conference

For Creatives

A gathering for Christian creatives
seeking renewal, clarity, and community.

The Well invites writers, speakers, artists, musicians, filmmakers, actors, and visionary creators into a place where inspiration runs deep and creative strength is restored.

Immerse yourself in worship, dynamic keynotes, hands-on workshops, industry training, and meaningful connections with a community that understands your calling.

Step into a space designed to equip your craft, refresh your spirit, and replenish your creative well, so your creativity flows freely.

Sessions:

Speaking, Writing, Art, Music,
Theater/Film, Marketing,
Personal Growth,
Biblical Studies

COUPON CODE
THEWELL50

Plus:

15-Minute Coaching Sessions
Sell in our Bookstore
Celebration of Arts
and More!

SEEYOUATTHEWELL.NET   THEWELLMINISTRYFORCREATIVES   SEEYOUATTHEWELL